Weavi

For Beginners

A Beginner's Guide to the Tools, Techniques and Basics of Home Spinning and Weaving so That You Can Easily Hand-Craft Beautiful Creations and Even Start a Home-Based Business

By Nora Amlani

Contents

Thank you for buying this book and I hope that you will find it useful. If you will want to share your thoughts on this book, you can do so by leaving a review on the Amazon page, it helps me out a lot.

Chapter 1: A Hobby or a New Trade?

Prior to rushing out to purchase supplies, it could be useful to ask yourself what you wish to achieve from finding out how to do weaving and spinning at home. Even if you are a newbie, you must not allow this to discourage you from huge plans! Weaving and spinning are rather simple to learn-- and whether you just desire an interesting brand-new pastime to do in your free time, or have ideas of turning it into a new trade, it is completely up to you!

If you choose to weave and spin entirely for your own entertainment, you have made an exceptional choice of a brand-new hobby. As quickly as you learn the fundamentals, you are going to be well on your path to developing lovely products to keep or to give as presents. You are going to have numerous hours of entertainment when you find out how to make your own cloth, yarn and vibrant creations that you can utilize for yourself or give to others.

Nevertheless, if having a little company of your own interests you, house spinning and weaving could be the perfect business endeavor. As each item you create is going to be special, you can provide consumers unique creations that they would never ever have the ability to locate in any shop. The aspect of individuality, plus the care you invest in creating homemade, quality items, can turn an enjoyable pastime into a lucrative business endeavor if you want to do so.

Whatever goal fits your preferences, the essential point to remember is to begin small. You desire every piece you make to be a stunning treasure. When you begin with the fundamentals and give yourself ample time to learn and hone your abilities, you are going to see your talents blooming in no time whatsoever

Why is home weaving and spinning so prominent today? There are a variety of reasons for this. Initially, increasingly more individuals today value quality. They are bored of mass-produced, generic items which do not last long. When you create each item by hand, one by one, you are not just making something great-- you are fastidiously producing quality.

Second, creating these items one at a time additionally leads to a unique item. If you have actually been disappointed with home furnishings and clothing that all appear identical, you understand why this is a problem. Home weaving and spinning implies that for every single item you create, there aren't any like it anywhere else.

Third, more individuals today value the essentials in life. They notice that the old-school ways of doing things actually are superior. Making cloth, yarn and dyeing, have actually all been around for hundreds of years. It is going to be like entering the past and noticing how great it is to bring it into today.

There is absolutely nothing quite like making beautiful things in the convenience of your own home. After you start, you are going to see how simple it is to make beautiful material beyond your craziest dreams. You might additionally be amazed by how easy it is to learn. You do not have to invest cash in taking classes so as to discover how to do it. When your family and friends see what you have actually made, they might want you to show them how to do it, as well!

Home weaving and spinning could be unwinding, interesting, and enjoyable! If you begin with little projects, you are going to undoubtedly be delighted with the outcomes! After you have actually grasped the essentials, you can carry on to bigger and more complex tasks. Whether you are currently quite knowledgeable about arts and crafts, or whether home weaving and spinning is your initial endeavor, when you have started, the opportunities are going to be almost endless. It is not going to take long for you to end up being an expert!

If you have a little bit of spare time, learning this craft is going to be certainly worth the effort. It is going to provide you numerous hours of pleasure, as you weave and spin in the convenience of home. The delight and pride you are going to have from the end products are going to be matched just by the wonder of everybody who looks at them. There are a couple of hobbies that provide so much.

The ease in which you could turn this pastime into a home-based business is an extra benefit. Whether you wish to make additional money from your own home or merely love the look on individuals' faces when they hold a special creation in their own hands, all it requires is a bit of practice to turn weaving and spinning as a pastime into an amazing method to earn money.

Even if you have actually never created anything by hand previously, you are going to discover this art easy to learn and enjoyable to do. Upon discovering this new ability, it is one that you can delight in for the remainder of your life. You are going to quickly see that it is a fantastic way to develop unique treasures. Each is going to be a special piece that you and everybody on your gift list are going to value and utilize with pride.

All you have to do is take the initial step to discover the essentials. You are going to quickly be creating the most beautiful things you have actually ever laid your eyes on-- all with your own 2 hands!

Chapter 2: What Do You Require to Start?

The ideal way to find out how to produce your own homemade items is to begin with the fundamentals. When you begin with the fundamental supplies, you are going to have what you require on-hand to learn this amazing brand-new craft. After you have actually found out the fundamentals of weaving and spinning, you can acquire extra supplies to produce excellent masterpieces. This chapter informs you what supplies you are going to require to start.

Supplies You Require

1. TABLE LOOM.

Table looms are offered in a variety of various sizes, so you can pick the loom that is most practical and comfy for you to utilize. When picking a table loom, you can select from one which is ready for you to utilize or one that you should assemble on your own. While a pre-assembled loom might cost a bit more, you might choose it is worth a couple of additional dollars.

2. LOOM TOOL AND ADD-ONS

In case you do not select a table loom with all of the essential tools, you could buy these products individually. These consist of lease sticks, apron rods, threading hooks, and tie-up cable. Accessories you are going to utilize for weaving consist of a stick shuttle, boat shuttle and a warping board.

3. WEAVING BENCH

A weaving bench is a more comfy, alternative to utilizing a free-standing loom.

4. LEGS FOR TABLE LOOM

If you choose not to utilize a weaving bench, you can acquire legs for your table loom rather. These legs are offered in various sizes, so you can select the length that is the most proper for you. Legs for table looms could be discovered in a range of woods; maple and cherry are among the most prominent.

5. YARN FOR WEAVING

Yarn for weaving could be bought in a wide variety of colors, so you can select your favorites for the items you want to make. Nevertheless, picking the best yarn is a lot more essential. The ply and weight you pick depend upon the weaving projects you intend to attempt. The two most typical types of yarn utilized for weaving are the Shetland Style yarn and Highland Style yarn. Both of these yarns are top quality, complete wool.

Supplies You Are Going To Have

1. SPINNING WHEEL

The spinning wheel is the biggest, most expensive, and most crucial item for spinning. When picking a spinning wheel, the quantity of area you have, and your own individual inclination, are as essential as the expense. The two primary spinning wheel styles are the Saxony style and the upright wheel.Spinning wheels are offered as double-drive wheels, single-drive wheels, and bobbin lead wheels.

2. DROP SPINDLE

When you are finding out how to spin, you can utilize a drop spindle rather than a conventional spinning wheel. If an expense is a problem, beginning with a drop spindle is more suitable. They are extremely affordable, and you could even create your own. A second reason for utilizing a drop spindle is that it is extremely little. Whether you have a restricted quantity of space in your house, or whether you desire a portable product to ensure that you can spin when you are far from home, a drop spindle is a perfect substitute for a full-sized spinning wheel.

3. CARDER

If you are going to be dealing with wool that isn't pre-cleaned and ready for usage, you are going to require a carder for this function. You can choose a drum carder or a hand carder.

4. FIBERS FOR SPINNING

You are going to additionally require fibers to start your brand-new craft. While there are several types of fibers offered, a few of the most prominent are angora, alpaca and flax. Novices typically discover flax to be a bit more complicated to utilize than these other prominent fibers.

When you are trying to find the supplies you are going to utilize for weaving and spinning, it is an excellent idea to do a bit of comparison-shopping. You can discover all the supplies you require at a great value. You do not have to invest a fortune to find out how to do your brand-new craft, or to get fantastic outcomes.

Nevertheless, if you desire your craft to be successful, you must not be lured to acquire supplies that are in less than ideal condition. Trying to make-do with used or old supplies could stand in the way of enjoying your brand-new endeavor, in addition to stopping you from creating quality items.

You must additionally not be lured to purchase more supplies than you require to start. After you have actually mastered weaving and spinning, you can constantly contribute to your supply collection when they are essential. The supplies noted in the parts above are going to get you well on your path to numerous hours of fun.

Chapter 3: Making Your Own Cloth

If you have actually never ever considered how cloth is created, you might be shocked at how basic the procedure really is. Although ending up being a specialist weaver is going to require practice, you can discover how to weave in extremely little time. When you understand the fundamentals, it ought to be enough for you to begin with excitement.

The cloth is created by the procedure referred to as weaving. Rugs, blankets, and comparable products are additionally created by this identical procedure. Weaving includes passing threads initially under and after that over one another. The kind of thread you utilize, and how firmly the threads are woven, determine the finished item. When explained in such an easy way, you ought to discover the idea of weaving simple to comprehend, and the procedure simple to do.

The primary loom purpose is to make the weaving procedure much simpler by holding both the unwoven threads and woven material. If you want, you might attempt to weave by hand initially, without utilizing the loom. You are going to see right away why utilizing a loom is more suitable!

There are 2 points to bear in mind before you start weaving. Initially, you might have heard the words wcft and warp, which are pointed out often when describing woven handicrafts. These terms refer to the thread positions when someone is weaving.

Second, the tighter the threads are positioned together during weaving, the heavier or thicker the finished item. If the threads are positioned together too loosely, or if they consist of spaces, it is going to decrease the end product quality.

When you are selecting a thread, you ought to choose one that is simple to manage. The easier you can handle the threads, the better your completed project is going to be. An extra, useful suggestion for the novice is to choose threads or yarns in 2 various colors. If you select one color for the weft and a contrasting color for the warp, it is going to make handling your threads a lot easier.

There are 4 primary procedures in the whole procedure of weaving. If you acquaint yourself with these ideas ahead of time, it is going to assist your weaving to continue a lot more efficiently. The procedures associated with weaving consist of:

- 1. Shedding

Shedding is the procedure where the warp yarns are lifted onto the loom. In case you are utilizing a contemporary loom for weaving, shedding is performed immediately by the loom itself. Appropriate shedding guarantees that the warp threads or yarns are situated properly to get the filling threads or yarns.

- 2. Selecting

Selecting is the procedure in which the shuttle properly inserts and places the filling threads or yarns.

- 3. Battening

After the filling yarn is placed, the loom's reed battens the particular yarns versus the fabric.

- 4. Taking up

As each section or area of fabric or material is finished, it needs to be "taken up." This indicates that it is wound onto a beam. You could carry on weaving without the completed material being in the way.

If this seems complex, it is truly not difficult whatsoever. You might have a couple of mistakes initially, however with a bit of practice, you could rapidly end up being an expert. The ideal general rule to bear in mind is to begin simply and make progress. After you have actually established the skill of weaving plain cloth, you can carry on to more complex tasks.

There is another fascinating point for you to think about when you are intending to begin weaving. Do you recall those small plastic looms that you or your buddies had when you were kids? If you resemble the majority of grownups today, you most likely spent lots of hours of your youth creating nice potholders from cloth bands in a rainbow of colors. The loom held the warp bands safely, as you inserted and placed the weft bands with a small hooks or with your fingers.Creating those potholders was the easiest kind of weaving-- so you are not truly a beginner to the procedure whatsoever!

The delight you sense in creating those potholders, and the pride you sense when you handed them away as presents, can return to life once again when you begin discovering how to weave on your contemporary loom!

You could start by weaving plain cloth with the yarn or thread, which you find the simplest to manage. You are going to undoubtedly be thrilled at how your initial projects end up. By creating sensible room for mistake, particularly in the start, you are going to take pride in your brand-new achievements.

After having a bit of practice with weaving, you can carry on to more complex projects. You might choose that you wish to weave blankets or rugs, to have for your own usage or to give as presents. There is absolutely nothing quite as remarkable, nor as valued, as hand-woven items for the house.

Along with weaving bigger and more complex items, you can additionally attempt your hand at weaving patterns. While this is not a good idea for the novice, it should not take a lot for you to be ready for this following action. Think of how delighted all of your family members and friends are going to be when they get special presents which you not just wove yourself but custom-made in charming patterns only for them!

Weaving has actually been a part of life for hundreds of years, in cultures all across the world. For some people, it was an essential part of life; for others, a pleasurable craft. It could be whatever you want it to be for you, today. Knowing how to weave cloth is just the start. You could make clothes, items for the home, and presents. You might have come far since the days of creating vibrant potholders on a plastic loom. However, the principle is the identical, and the procedure is almost as easy. You might have had the standard understanding, talent, and abilities for weaving without even recognizing it!

Now that you understand how straightforward it is to create your own cloth, all you have to do is get your brand-new loom and your preferred yarn or thread and start! You are going to quickly see stunning treasures appearing right ahead of you!

Chapter 4: Creating Your Yarn

If you like knitted clothes and other items, you are going to like discovering how to create your own yarn. Whether you start with wool in its natural, initial state, or begin with ready-to-go materials, you are going to quickly look at spinning as an amazing adventure.

The procedure of creating yarn depends upon the kind of wheel you have actually acquired. If you have actually chosen to have a go at drop spindle initially, you are going to be surprised at how rapidly and quickly yarn could be made. The procedure of utilizing a drop spindle is the following:

- Tying the leader.

The leader is a yarn piece which is roughly eighteen inches in length. You start by connecting this yarn piece onto the spindle. It is then bound around the spindle and looped to ensure that it is going to hold safely.

- Spinning.

Gradually and thoroughly rotate clockwise while turning the spindle, having the fiber in one hand and the spindle in another.

- Winding On.

This is the procedure in which the newly-created fiber starts to wind the spindle up. It ought to continue effortlessly, with no gaps or looseness.

- Joining Fiber.

You can put on extra fiber by overlapping fresh wool across the freshly-made yarn. As it twists into the initial leader thread, it is going to end up being firmly connected as if it were one piece.

With this simple, fast approach, you are discovering how to create your own yarn!

If you have actually chosen to utilize a conventional spinning wheel to create yarn, the procedure is additionally rather easy. The precise procedure relies on the particular kind of spinning wheel that you have actually picked.

You might additionally select between "spinning in the grease" or utilizing wool, that has actually currently been cleaned and carded. Carding is the procedure of mixing the fiber to make it consistent and smooth. Spinning in the grease suggests that the wool has actually not yet been cleaned, and still includes natural lanolin. Whichever form you utilize is generally a question of individual preference.

A single-drive spinning wheel is the kind of standard spinning wheel simplest for a newbie to operate. If you currently understand how to utilize a sewing device, you are going to discover a single-drive spinning wheel to be fairly comparable.

When utilizing a single-drive spinning wheel, the speed is managed by a different bobbin brake. All it requires is a bit of practice to identify if the speed is precise.

An additional benefit of utilizing a single-drive spinning wheel is that it enables you to set the flyer and bobbin tensions individually. If you do not currently have any experience with running a spinning wheel, this could prove to be really helpful.

When utilizing a spinning wheel which needs treadling, it is necessary to keep the movements of your feet consistent and even. If you are not knowledgeable about the term, treadling describes making use of foot pedals.

Each flyer rotation twists the fiber and includes a twist to the finished yarn piece. This procedure contributes to both the consistency and strength of the completed product. When it is twisted equally, the completed yarn is going to be smooth and devoid of flaws.

If you want, yarn could be colored prior to getting started spinning, or after it is completed. You might like it in its initial state. Natural yarn could be rather lovely-- and a lot more so when you have produced the completed item on your own!

No matter the kind of spinning approach you have actually selected, you are certainly going to be impressed with the outcomes! You might currently be considering all the usages you have for your freshly-created yarn. Some terrific ideas about projects you can create are going to be in an approaching chapter. Before you continue, there are a couple of more things you may like to understand about creating your own yarn.

While flax is a plant that grows freely, there are 2 other typical yarn sources. The artificial material might be to your taste. If not, you might choose natural wool. Angora, alpaca and other natural wools originate from animals. When these animals are kept by trustworthy people, they are not hurt by utilizing their wool for spinning.

Shearing the wool from these animals is a totally pain-free operation, and their wool grows back naturally later. Even the most diligent animal-lover ought to have no qualms about utilizing this sort of wool. In fact, lots of people these days who do spinning as a trade have their own animals, when space and time allows. This is the way it was normally carried out in the old days.

For the most part, the yarn you can locate in your neighborhood shops is artificial. While there is absolutely nothing bad with artificial yarn, the reality that it includes manmade materials might motivate you to value natural products a lot more.

Additionally, that which you locate online or in stores is most likely to have been mass-produced. When you start to create your own yarn, you are going to discover the distinction. As one of the most essential and nicest parts of creating something on your own is that each of your productions is unique, this is definitely correct when you spin your yarn. Each completed strand is going to be something extra-special-- something that you, yourself, have actually produced.

There is absolutely nothing that can compare to the sensation you are going to have when you look at the yarn that you have actually created with your own hands. The bright side is that there is a lot more to find out and more to choose. Should you leave your yarn as it naturally it, or attempt dyeing? What could you do with the yarn you have created after you have admired how stunning it is? Creating your own yarn is quite an achievement, however, responses to these questions and more are in the next chapters!

Chapter 5: Everything about Dyeing

Natural is stunning, however the color can absolutely be more remarkable! Whether you intend to make items from your spun yarn or woven cloth or whether you wish to appreciate it as-is, you are going to see how many more choices you have when you find out everything about dyeing.

Dyeing is extremely easy, however, if you desire the very best outcomes, you want to understand some truths beforehand. While it is a simple procedure, all it requires is a little error to lead to a catastrophe. If you have actually had any unfavorable experiences with dye in the past, you currently understand how challenging it is to get rid of unwanted dye-- not just from a fabric, however from your skin and your house. With a little understanding, care and caution, dyeing could be an enjoyable experience with stunning outcomes.

There are 2 fundamental sorts of dye. The natural dye originates from plants. Synthetic dye offers you the option of many more colors, and the dye lasts a lot longer wherever it is used.

The kind of dye you select depends upon the material where you intend to use it. Standard dye works ideally for acrylic, and acid dyes are better for wool items, and disperse dye is frequently utilized on polyester. Cotton could react to any of these types of dye. Individuals who are specifically environmentally friendly sometimes utilize food coloring.

When you have actually picked the kind of dye most suitable to your product, you additionally should keep in mind the material's porousness. The more porous a product is, the faster it is going to take in a dye. This impacts the hue of the color and strength. For instance, a material that is extremely porous is going to soak up more dye quicker, leading to a much darker, deeper color than a less porous material. You need to take this into consideration so as to accomplish the wanted impact.

The dye could be discovered in the forms of a dye paste or dye solution. While a liquid dye solution is normally most proper for vat dyeing, a dye paste is simpler to utilize when you want to apply a dye manually.

Utilizing a liquid dye solution in a vat is frequently ideal when administering single-color dye to a big piece of material. A dye paste could be utilized if you wish to have a variety of various design patterns, colors or have just a little bit of material to dye. Using a mordant after dyeing is going to assist the dye to remain in place.

In addition to these fundamental types of dyeing, there are 2 other techniques that are both rather popular. The simpleness of these techniques, along with their gorgeous, unique results, accounts for their prevalent appeal. You do not have to be a specialist or have any special understanding to attempt either of these approaches.

- Tie-Dyeing.

If you have actually attempted tie-dyeing before, you currently understand how simple it is to do. After you have actually woven your own cloth, you could get a fantastic impact from tie-dyeing. The simplest procedure of tie-dyeing needs absolutely nothing more than an elastic band and a vat in which to dye the material. All you have to do is connect the rubber bands in loops in your fabric and dye it based upon the particular directions. You are going to certainly concur that tie-dyeing cloth that you have actually created yourself supplies gorgeous outcomes.

- Batik.

Another prominent kind of dyeing is called batik. You have actually most likely seen all the things from clothing to household items in shops, yet not understood how they were created. You might not have actually understood how simple it is to create batik yourself. It is a really easy method to create one of a kind productions.

To create batik, the only additional items you are going to require are a mix of beeswax and paraffin. Both of these items could be discovered in a hobby or specialty shops. Begin by administering this mix to your tidy, dry fabric. You need to offer the wax enough time to dry and cool on the material before dyeing. If you are in a rush, you can put the material in the fridge. This is going to enable the wax to dry much quicker.

When you position your fabric in the dye, the wax is going to break naturally, enabling the dye to create patterns on the material. The length of time your project stays in the dye relies on the particular kind of material you have and the sort of dye you are utilizing. In-depth directions ought to come with the dye when you buy it.

After your product is dyed, you need to get rid of the wax mix. The most convenient and the cleanest way to do this is to put your material in between pages of the fade-resistant paper. It is necessary to utilize a newspaper printed with ink that is not going to come off on your fabric. When the fabric is in place, thoroughly iron it. This is going to induce the wax to liquify.

The completed item needs to be completely yet thoroughly cleaned up. You do not desire any wax residue to stay on your material. Utilizing a mild soap is going to get rid of the staying wax, and leave you with the most gorgeous item you have ever laid your eyes on.

Prior to starting any dyeing project, it is an excellent idea to have suitable cleansers on hand. Many individuals who dye regularly feel that standard bleach is the very best. You are going to want to clean the vat and any other materials that you have actually utilized, along with having the ability to tidy and sterilize your skin or any other locations which might have been impacted by spills or splatters.

Regardless of how much you like natural yarn, cloth and other materials, you ought to attempt each of these dyeing approaches at least one time. Even if you are a newbie, the outcomes are going to be impressive.

The best part of any type of dyeing is that regardless of what you create, it is going to be unique. It could turn even the simplest, common material into an amazing masterpiece. The absolute best part of it is that you are going to understand that you created it yourself. There is absolutely nothing rather like a unique, handcrafted production. It is something that you are going to wear with pride or give to a special individual as a present.

Chapter 6: What Do You Wish to Make?

Project Ideas

Whether you have been practicing weaving and spinning and have actually ended up being a professional at your brand-new craft, or whether you are still a novice who is finding out these fantastic abilities and anticipating future objectives, you may like to think of certain ideas for projects you can create. All of these projects need just a moderate level of ability, and some are really simple to do. They are enjoyable ways to include what you have actually found out.

If you have actually delighted in weaving cloth, you are going to find weaving a rug to be much more amazing. Even though this project is done by a comparable procedure, you are not going to require a loom. Rather, all you are going to require to weave a rug is a rug frame. A rug frame is a low-cost item that you can locate in lots of hobby or specialty shops. If you wish to conserve cash, you can even create a rug frame on your own.

Weaving a rug could be simpler than weaving cloth. With simply a bit of practice, you can create a charming rug within a couple of hours. Comparing all of these elements to the pricey, mass-produced rugs you locate in stores ought to be an excellent incentive to attempt creating your initial rug. Not just is it cost-effective, your completed rug is going to be unique. The patterns, styles and designs you select are totally up to you!

Your weaving abilities can additionally encompass creating blankets. If you have actually ever seen and appreciated standard Native American blankets and wished that you had the skill to create them yourself, now you are able to! You can start with an easy pattern, and progress to more detailed designs.

Dyeing fabric is an easy to do ability with almost unlimited possibilities. Whether you utilize a cloth that you have actually created yourself or material that you buy, you could design and develop distinct items in just a number of hours. The opportunities vary from developing and dyeing clothing to creating and dyeing curtains for your house, and a lot, lot more. You are going to locate more chances for dyeing than there are colors in the rainbow!

The yarn has actually been a special item for women and girls across the generations. Actually, some guys delight in dealing with yarn as much as the women do. One standard favorite for dealing with yarn is knitting. Maybe you have actually attempted it yourself, or have actually seen older women in your household as they knitted. You could knit baby booties and blankets, headscarfs and mittens for everybody in your family. Knitted products aren't just beautiful, they are additionally very warm!

The other conventional technique of dealing with yarn is crocheting. Crocheting has actually ended up being significantly popular throughout the last couple of decades. One explanation behind this is that crocheting is extremely easy. Even a kid can do it. You could crochet sweaters, caps, blankets and numerous other good items. As a crochet yarn and hook are portable, you could take your crocheting work with you to deal with when you have leisure time.

A modern approach of crocheting is with using a granny square. You merely crochet a granny square in whichever size is suitable for your project and carry on by creating however many squares you require. When you have the variety of squares you want, you can stitch the squares together. This is a simple way to make even the biggest afghan in a brief amount of time.

The yarn you have actually created can additionally be utilized for braiding. Braiding is performed by linking 3 yarn strands. The strands could be doubled if you desire heavier or thicker braids. They could be all the identical color or various colors, based upon the result you desire.

Braids have numerous useful functions. Among the most prominent is to hold hanging baskets. These baskets could be utilized to hold plants or other products. Hanging baskets with handcrafted braids are a wonderful method to make any space brilliant and fresh.

Handcrafted braids can additionally be utilized to make crafts like photo frames. They are lasting, durable, and practically unbreakable. They additionally appear much better than the frames you can purchase in a shop.

These are simply a few of the ways you can put your brand-new skills into practical usage. As soon as you have actually ended up being familiar with producing items with your own 2 hands, you are most likely going to wish to attempt everything that you have time to create. Even if you are still finding out the arts of weaving and spinning, you can create stunning items. Whatever you make is going to be totally distinct. Most importantly, you are going to see that hand-crafting is something that constantly holds your interest due to the fact that it is a lot of fun!

Chapter 7: Taking care of Your Materials

You might recognize with the old saying, "A great workman constantly takes great care of his tools." This holds true for your weaving and spinning tools, as well. The greater condition you maintain your supplies in, the longer they are going to last, and the better they are going to function.

Looking after your materials is easy. With the majority of your supplies, it is absolutely nothing more than good sense. Keeping them tidy, without debris, and kept securely when not being used is the only care that the majority of your supplies need.

Certain supplies do require some additional attention. You ought to thoroughly inspect your loom regularly to be certain that it has actually not built up any rust. You could clean your loom's metal parts with a typical sewing-machine oil. This is going to assist in making sure that your loom carries on running effortlessly.

Linseed or lemon oil could be utilized to keep your wood's loom fresh and clean. Some individuals discover linseed oil a bit challenging to handle. However, both work similarly well.

Lemon oil is additionally exceptional for cleaning your spinning wheel. As maintaining your spinning wheel in great working order implies keeping it correctly preserved, you ought to ensure to clean it regularly.

Both a loom and a spinning wheel ought to be inspected regularly to be certain that all of the parts are in place. Parts need to be changed whenever they start to wear out. Utilizing a loom or spinning wheel with parts which are worn out can harm your whole device, along with making it less reliable.

Dyes require a specific degree of care, additionally. Initially, if you have dyes that are no longer in exceptional condition you ought to get rid of them. In case they are kept too long, they can weaken. Their composition can alter, and they are no longer going to work. Your material might be destroyed if you attempt to utilize dye that isn't fresh any longer.

Second, many dyes lose their effectiveness after they have actually been opened. If you just utilize a part of a dye, deal with the rest. Regardless of sort of dye it is, appropriate disposal is necessary. The initial package ought to supply guidelines on how to deal with it securely.

Taking care of your products additionally indicates keeping them out of your kids' hands. Certain supplies have the potential to be hazardous to kids. Kids, on the other hand, can quickly destroy your supplies. While teaching them not to have fun with your weaving and spinning materials is necessary, guaranteeing that they are not available to your children without your guidance is similarly essential. As animals can present the identical problems as kids, they must not be allowed close to your supplies. It could be useful to create space where you do your weaving and spinning off-limits to young kids and pets. This fundamental decision can stop unneeded mishaps from taking place.

When not being used, your weaving and spinning supplies could be securely kept where they are not going to be disrupted. A space or big closet that is devoid of wetness, dust, and other residue is ideal. It is a great strategy to have coverings for your spinning wheel and loom, if feasible.

Keeping your supplies tidy, safe, and in good shape is the ideal method to have them all set for several years of use. The tiny amount of time it requires to care for your supplies is certainly worth it. When you do not need to fret about damaged or harmed supplies, you can concentrate on enjoying them. With simply a bit of effort, you could enjoy them for several years.

Chapter 8: Taking care of the Products You Created

Handcrafted items are the most fantastic ones. When you have actually created something on your own, it means a good deal to you. Putting a bit of more time into taking care of these items suggests that you are going to have and enjoy them for a very long time.

Maintaining your handmade items in good shape indicates protecting their quality and their distinct appeal. Luckily, it is simple to do this. All it needs is a bit of special attention to your item.

Yarns, and products created from yarn, need to be cleaned by hand constantly. Under no conditions can yarn be cleaned in a washing machine, or a clothes dryer. Either of these appliances is going to destroy yarn totally, inducing it to shrink and end up being out of shape. Rather, clean your yarn items in cool water, with the mildest soap you can discover. You could additionally utilize Woolite, which is specifically created for cleaning up fragile fabrics. It is really affordable and could be discovered in almost any shop.

Drying yarn items additionally needs some unique care. The most convenient and best method to dry products created from yarn is to permit them to naturally air-dry on something flat. Wet yarn products ought to never be hung up with clothespins, on a clothesline.or on hangersTrying to dry them by these techniques is going to induce them to extend and be yanked out of shape. While a flat surface might take more to dry the item, your handmade productions are going to remain in their initial shape and keep their lovely shape. It is reckless to utilize an iron on products created from yarn.

Clothing or other articles which have actually been dyed require a little additional care. Powerful detergents ought to be stayed clear of, no matter the material, as they could induce the colors to fade. Bleach must never ever be utilized on dyed materials. Dyed clothing and other items are going to additionally hold their intense color more if they are not dried in powerful, direct sunshine. If the material allows, they could be dried in a clothes dryer, or outside far from powerful sunshine.

Utilizing an iron on dyed clothes can induce the dye to fade, specifically if it is performed regularly. If it is essential to iron your dyed clothes, you ought to utilize the coolest setting you can, and just iron them when you have to. Whenever you can, it is better to enable wrinkles to be removed naturally during drying. Dyed clothes not having yarn could be dried on a clothing line or on a hanger.

If you have actually created blankets or rugs, keeping them as tidy as feasible is going to assist in preventing the requirement for regular cleaning. When they do have to be cleaned up, you ought to select the technique ideal for the specific material. Woolite, or another comparable moderate item, could work effectively for washing blankets and rugs. As blankets and rugs are big, drying them on a clothing line is advised, unless they are created from yarn. Handmade blankets and rugs do not react good to a clothes dryer, so it is ideal to stay away from this approach.

Woolite is additionally an excellent option for cleaning woven cloth. While moderate cleaning agent is not going to harm most sorts of cloth, Woolite is going to aid it to remain fresher, brighter and in better condition.

You have actually put time and effort into producing charming items. It is just normal for you to wish for them to remain in ideal condition for a lot of time. When they look as great as when you initially created them, your handmade productions are going to bring you several years of pleasure and pride. Putting a little additional time into their correct care is definitely worth it. Whatever you make is going to be a thing to treasure for several years. You might even discover that your handmade items end up being mementos and treasures to thrill future generations. All it requires is some additional care to protect them in their initial, lovely shape.

Chapter 9: What To Do With Your Creations?

You might have created lots of great products, or are considering ones which you wish to create. You might be wondering how many enjoyable and useful uses there are for your creations. If you resemble many people who spin, dye and weave, the more great utilizations you have for your items, the more you are going to delight in creating them.

One usage for your items is to enjoy them on your own. Besides, you have actually put your time and effort into discovering these crafts, and much more time into practice, so it is just normal for you to enjoy a few of the rewards.

You could create your own clothing if you want to do so. As soon as you have actually seen how unique and distinct your handmade cloth is, you understand that it is much better than anything you can discover in a shop. Similarly crucial, every article of clothes you create is unique. Regardless of what pattern, color or style you select, there is absolutely nothing quite like it anywhere.

You can additionally make home furnishings for your home. Rugs, batik wall-hangings and blankets are going to look fantastic in any room of your home. They are going to offer an air of uniqueness, as they were all created specifically by you.

While enjoying your own productions is terrific, you likely do not wish to keep them all to yourself. Part of the enjoyment of developing special items is to share them with other individuals. A number of the items you create are perfect for giving as presents. Whether you are considering Christmas, baby showers, birthdays, or "just because," absolutely nothing is going to make your recipients feel as unique as a present which you have actually created by hand.

Creating homemade presents has an advantage. If you have actually ever had a problem choosing what sort of present to offer to somebody on a special occasion, this is going to no longer be an issue when you pick to give your homemade crafts. Rather than going for presents that are not quite suitable, you can custom-make every present separately for every fortunate recipient.

Gift-giving with handmade items is constantly better than buying products from a shop. Sizes, patterns, colors, and styles are all up to you to choose. You could be guaranteed that everyone you provide with your handicrafts is going to value and treasure something you created only for them.

When all of your buddies and members of your household look at your productions, their thrilling reactions might provide you the idea of turning your brand-new free-time hobby into a successful home-based business. While beginning your own business does need some mindful thought and preparation, it does not have to be hard at all.

There are a variety of alternatives for beginning a trade with weaving and spinning. You can create the products, and after that, have them offered in a consignment store. The majority of big cities have several of these stores. If you pick this approach, the things you make are going to be completely up to you. You could create however many products you want, and whichever kind you delight in creating the most.

Another choice is to promote for special orders. When you are positive in your capabilities, you can put an advertisement in a widely-circulated magazine or newspaper or on social media. You can additionally begin a site to promote your productions. If you select this approach, do not be amazed if your brand-new home-based business starts to build extremely rapidly. The mix of products being created by hand and made to order is incredibly popular. Clients like the idea of choosing an item they desire and having it specifically created only for them. You might even acquire more consumers when individuals who purchase your products show them off to all of their buddies.

There is another useful, enjoyable use for your creations. It is something that you might not have actually considered previously. There are lots of charities and groups consistently in requirement of assistance. You could do a fantastic service for your community by thinking about the possibilities.

One idea is to offer your homemade items for fundraising raffles. In lots of neighborhoods, this is frequently done at yearly fairs or other occasions. You could approach an organization which you are familiar with and inquire if they would want several of your items for their raffles. When the earnings go straight to these sort of deserving causes, you are going to feel motivated by your contribution. You are going to additionally understand that your workmanship has actually been put to great use.

Another idea is to provide your productions to agencies that assist the less lucky. Many big cities have shelters for homeless persons, services for youth, and special residences for battered women. It doesn't require a lot of effort to learn what sort of agencies are near you. It is among the ideal methods in which you could aid individuals in their time of need.

All of these types of agencies are often in need of blankets, clothing and other comparable products. They typically depend on donations, that are typically insufficient to assist all of the individuals they serve. If you can create some additional sweaters, blankets and other clothing articles, you are going to be supplying a terrific service for guys, women, and kids who are less lucky and experiencing a challenging time.

There are numerous things that you could do with your creations. After you have actually ended up being a professional in weaving, spinning, and dyeing, you might discover that you enjoy creating certain types of items or utilizing specific techniques more than others. You might even choose that you wish to focus on one of them. This is an indication that you have actually refined your strategies, and have actually grown to like your brand-new craft. It is additionally an indication that your weaving, spinning and other workmanship has the capacity of ending up being far more than a part-time pastime. Whether you select to start your own home-based business, make fantastic contributions to a preferred charity, or just thrill all of your family members and friends, you can now do just that.

Weaving and spinning is not a challenging art form to learn. It does not call for a lot of expenditure. All it truly demands is the dedication to practice, to learn and to perfect till you are totally pleased with the outcomes. The pleasure you get from creating individual handiwork is your finest guarantee of this satisfaction coming quickly. Weaving and spinning are going to feel like a natural component of your life really quickly after you have actually started learning.

In case you have taken the initiative to purchase and go through this book, you are currently on your path to several years of a craft that is going to absolutely improve your life. With a bit of time, you are certainly on your path to succeeding!

I hope that you enjoyed reading through this book and that you have found it useful. If you want to share your thoughts on this book, you can do so by leaving a review on the Amazon page. Have a great rest of the day.

Printed in Great Britain
by Amazon